The Art of

The TRUMP

ISBN-13:978-1541382367

ISBN-10:1541382366

The Art of the TRUMP

Contents

Introduction

This book is dedicated to the greatness, innovation, creativity, sacrifice, hard work, resilience, and inner strength that IS America and the high principles that most Americans continue to uphold.

The election of President Donald J. Trump as the 45th President of the United States of America is a clear mandate from its minority electorate who demand a drastic reversal to the liberal political status quo in America.

Political pundits ponder what changes to government policies and to governance President Trump will enact during his first, and likely second term that will forever change the faces of Americans. How will most Americans view President Trump as our leader, how will they feel about our nation, will there be a resultant cultural revolution, and what will be the future impact of a Trump America on the global economy?

How will President Trump's popularity rise as he leads Americans to greater prosperity? Will Trump become the first King or Emperor of the United States of America? President Trump is the first multi-billionaire to win the White House, and he brings to the office his diverse business interests and contacts all over the world. How will the art of the Trump be revealed? When will the trumpets sound, if at all?

Disclaimer

The observations, opinions, conjecture, predictions and representations in this book, while partially based on various sources such as biographical materials, news stories, and other information in the public domain, are meant to continue a public discourse as guaranteed by the U.S. Constitution's 1st Amendment, Freedom of the Press and Free Speech.

There is no intent or desire to disparage or discredit the obvious apex successes Mr. Donald J. Trump has achieved, including the top prize, that being the American presidency. In fact, President Trump has many expert talents and skills that will serve him well as the apex leader of the free world.

The great sacrifices of Americans during all its wars, but particularly during the U.S. Civil War (by both sides) have served to uphold the U.S. Constitution by having one nation under one President at a time. No matter what candidate for the 2016 Presidency anyone may have supported, we trust President Trump with Godspeed in elevating Americans to greater financial attainments. We also hope to patch up old political wounds to permit Americans to be more united as we look optimistically into the event horizon.

This book was first published on New Years Day, 2017 before Presidential-Elect Donald Trump was inaugurated. This version contains a few updated observations and remarks.

Chapter 1
The Art of the Deal

President Trump has been somewhat of a puzzle to professional political observers, but not to his constituents. What are President Donald J. Trump's core beliefs that we can discern from his business and philosophy? He states in his bestselling book, *The Art of the Deal*, "I never go into negotiations thinking I'm going to lose." What else does President Trump believe that is likely to influence his political decision making?

1. Think big

"I like thinking big. I always have. To me it's very simple: if you're going to be thinking anyway, you might as well think big."

2. Protect the downside and the upside will take care of itself

"I always go into the deal anticipating the worst. If you plan for the worst--if you can live with the worst--the good will always take care of itself."

3. Maximize the options

"**I never get too attached to one deal or one approach**...I keep a lot of balls in the air, because most deals fall out, no matter how promising they seem at first."

4. Know your market

"I like to think that I have that instinct. That's why I don't hire a lot of number-crunchers, and I don't trust fancy marketing surveys. I do my own surveys and draw my own conclusions."

5. Use your leverage

"The worst thing you can possibly do in a deal is seem desperate to make it. That makes the other guy smell blood, and then you're dead."

6. Enhance your location

"Perhaps the most misunderstood concept in all of real estate is that the key to success is location, location, location...First of all, you don't necessarily need the best location. What you need is the best deal."

7. Get the word out

"One thing I've learned about the press is that they're always hungry for a good story, and the more sensational the better...The point is that if you are a little different, a little outrageous, or if you do things that are bold or controversial, the press is going to write about you."

8. Fight back

"In most cases I'm very easy to get along with. I'm very good to people who are good to me. But when people treat me badly or unfairly or try to take advantage of me, my general attitude, all my life, **has been to fight back very hard."**

9. Deliver the goods

"You can't con people, at least not for long. You can create excitement, you can do wonderful promotion and get all kinds of press, and you can throw in a little hyperbole. But if you don't deliver the goods, people will eventually catch on."

10. Contain the costs

"I believe in spending what you have to. But I also believe in not spending more than you should."

11. Have fun

"The real excitement is playing the game."

—

Chapter 2
The Art of the Steal

President Trump has stated during his run for the White House that the "system is rigged!" Let's look at the statistics to verify his prior criticism of the American voting system. The final popular vote count was almost 66 million for Hillary Clinton and about 63 million votes for Donald Trump. Were the U.S.A. a democratic system, Clinton would have become the first female President of the United States of America.

Clinton received 65,844,610 votes, or 48.2% of the total vote. Trump received 62,979,636 votes, or 46.1% of the total vote. (That's a difference of 2.86 million votes.) Were the U.S.A. an Electoral Democracy, Hillary Clinton would have won the election by popular mandate. However, America is a Constitutional Republic where the electorate actually votes to elect electors to the Electoral College. Now, if that's redundant and confusing, this is a fact that escapes most Americans who didn't pay enough attention during their high school American History classes. When we take a closer look at the creation of traditional voting districts, we find many strange and creative shapes to maximize the voting strength of certain groups over others due to migration, gerrymandering, and through actions of local and state politics.

In this latest round of peaceful elections subsequent to the American Civil War, it is blatantly clear that the *Democratic* candidate would have won if America were to be a pure **democracy**. However, a *Republican* won because the U.S.A. is a constitutional **republic**. This is not the first or last time a presidential candidate of the voting minority has won the top job in America due to the Electoral College system that was designed to insure political stability of the status quo. What we Americans and the world are waiting to learn is what is Donald Trump, President of the United States of America, will do to implement his personal beliefs, philosophy, and fate.

In many developing nations that have a history of autocracies, such as those that typify parts of the Middle-East, Asia, and South America, peaceful transition of power is not their typical political systems. Too often, military juntas by strong men overthrow legitimate civilian governments, or the reins of power pass through the blood line of its ruling families or ruling class. The United States of America is indeed a remarkable and stable political system, whereby there has been only one attempt by political opponents to the status quo to secede from the Union during the American Civil War.

The American electorate appears to favor periodic change from decade to decade, generation to generation, and after 8 years of Republican governance by President George W. Bush, they handed the keys to the White House to President Barrack Obama, who is handing over the top spot to President Donald J. Trump in another peaceful transition.

—

Chapter 3
The Art of the Real

Supporters of Hillary Clinton were shocked and awed by Donald Trump's supposedly unlikely path to the White House, so the conventional wisdom of most political pundits and media pre-election polls. Now, we are in a potentially new world order that will likely be precipitated by President Trump on many fronts, if we believe he will in most parts deliver on his electioneering statements.

Based on President Trump's political rhetoric, "tweets" and news media recording of everything Trump, here's what we could expect to various degrees of success on issues that are important to the American populace, and particularly to the voters who elected electors to the Electoral College who elected and elevated Mr. Donald J. Trump to be President of the United States of America, the most powerful and most prosperous nation in the history of mankind.

Let's compare the polar differences between the two major American political parties:

Republican's Agenda	Democrat's Agenda
Aggressive foreign policy	Global cooperation
Pro-war	Anti-war
Pro-life	Pro-abortion choice

Anti-immigration	Pro-immigration
Pro-patriotism	Anti-jingoism
Pro-smaller government	Pro-government expansion
Anti-budget deficit spending	Pro-deficit spending
Pro-private charities	Pro-government intervention
Pro-Christian God	Diverse religious views
Pro-elitism and exclusion	Pro-inclusion and equality
Anti-entitlement programs	Pro-entitlement programs
Pro-big business	Pro-small businesses
Pro-U.S. Hegemony	Shared global responsibility

During President Obama's two terms, he implemented an anti-war foreign policy that emphasized shared global policing and external national security responsibilities with American allies to form coalitions as an integral aspect of nation building, particularly in Moslem nations.

Domestically, Obama supported the "Dream Act" that gave the children of undocumented residents federal financial aid for college, and proposed "a path to citizenship" to "illegal aliens". The extension of many entitlement programs to non-citizens that weren't available to American citizens angered white middle-class taxpayers. The Obama Administration permitted the continuation of deficit spending, with a sizeable portion to support social entitlement programs that resulted in more government expansion.

Obama had a knack to downplay excessive patriotism and instead appealed for cooperation without using jingoism. Obama appeared more as a global voice, rather than solely an American one because while he is a publically declared Christian who attended church on Sundays, he practiced Islam during significant portion of his childhood while he lived with his mother and step-father in Indonesia. Consequently, he has an understanding and compassion for Moslems and is a true advocate of religious diversity and freedom. President Obama took liberal positions in the pro-life issue that was a moral issue to religious conservatives. He supported the idea of the woman's right to choose the death of her fetus, up to and including horrible late term abortions of viable babies.

Obama continued the liberal paradigm of government intervention to assist the poor, inclusion of greater numbers of minorities in government roles, and supported the success of small businesses while prosecuting big business for excesses.

Republicans since President Ronald Regan have supported an aggressive U.S. hegemony in foreign policy to protect America's global financial and security interests, up to and including open warfare with its adversaries, without the necessity to seek partnerships with other nations. Republican Presidents tend to draw heavily on pro-patriotic jingoism, support a strong and well-financed military-industrial complex, and aren't shy to push for large military budgets.

Conservatives are pro-balanced budgets, a sizeable retrenchment in social welfare programs and the resultant reduction in the size of government. Republicans desire to emphasize white majoritarian culture and its homogeneity by the exclusion of Mexican immigration through a boarder wall and the massive deportation of undocumented residents.

Republicans are passionate about the exercise of their religious views through supporting their churches, private charities, corporate giving, and pro-life positions. They care little for the inclusion of non-Christians of color into positions of power in the political and bureaucratic system. At times, it may appear the white male electorate that was the primarily key to electing Trump to be the President were angry at the status quo that favored minority and gender causes, which were often an affront to the white majority residing in America's Heartland and in the Southern States.

Republicans are the party representing "hands off" pro-business sentiments, whether large corporate interests or small business entrepreneurism. Christian and family values are hallmarks claimed by Republicans who believe life begins at inception, and women do not have reproductive rights that include the termination of pregnancy. Rather, most religious conservatives feel women must carry their unborn fetuses to term, and have the choice to give them up for adoption. Women's choice should not be abortion, but rather the choice to keep their babies or to give them up to private charities who will find them forever adoptive homes.

The question that concerns and intrigues both parties is whether President Trump, who criticized, fought and bucked the Republican Party during his unassisted historical run to 1400 Pennsylvania Avenue and who was once a registered Democrat and friend to Bill and Hillary Clinton, will implement policies that generally reflect Republican or Democratic ideals, something in between, or perhaps more likely, something unforeseen that demonstrates his "gut reactions" to issues.

Certainly, controlling immigration through deportation and other barriers is what President Trump's electorate fully expect from electioneering promises. Perhaps a Republican Congress will enact immigration policies to limit the total population percentage of non-white citizens to 30%, thereby insuring the white mainstream culture and political power will prevail over immigrants from all over the world who typically don't share common ideals with homegrown Americans.

White Americans are tired of entitlement programs that favor minorities and immigrants, both legal and illegal ones. Why should non-white groups benefit from tax dollars that the white majority contributes to government, when their own children don't receive the same equal playing field? Why is it considered racism and discrimination when whites want to have their own television network without colored people, while ethnic and racial minorities have media that caters only to their own groups, to the exclusion of whites? White Americans see themselves as unequal under the law.

Chapter 4
The Art of the Feel

Bill Clinton stated to the news media after his wife's unexpected loss to President Trump that he (Trump) was elected by angry white men. Hillary Clinton supporters insisted Trump won due to hatred due to their electoral expressions of racism. While the losers griped about winning the popular vote by almost 3 million votes, the largest gap in American history where the winner of the majority vote still lost the election, the reality is Donald Trump tapped into the undercurrent of how white voters in the Bible Belt, South, and Heartland really felt about the direction America had been taken by Obama, who opined that he could have beaten Trump had he been eligible for a 3rd term.

Why did an African American elected to 2 terms who was not supported by traditional Republicans who supported Trump in this election cycle? Trump won because he galvanized the conservative and anti-Obama vote, and African Americans who lived in the South and Industrial states didn't come out in large enough numbers to change the Electoral College votes for those swing states that could have gone to Hillary, had they ardently supported Clinton like Obama. The reality is American is divided along racial lines that reflect different cultural values, as "birds of a feather tend to flock together."

What did President Trump know about his constituency that Hillary did not? Here's a list of what most white Americans (particularly so-called angry white males) were concerned about:

- America, a country founded by white men, and whose descendants shed their blood in all its wars, has been under siege and becoming a nation ruled by its minorities who are projected to become the majority by mid-century if immigration controls and deportations are not enacted soon.

- American jobs have been exported to other countries, particularly to China and Mexico for more than a generation that has destroyed the manufacturing sector, particularly from areas that have historically provided steady good paying jobs for white men.

- The media has constantly pushed for more minority inclusion, interracial themes, and the expansion of minority cultures and their values. The rise of hip hop, rap, and other pop music genres has overshadowed the traditional love of country music that had defined majoritarian white culture for generations.

- Conservative white voters want to return to the 1950's prior to equal rights legislation, when society reflected traditional American values and television programs primarily depicted white life and culture portrayed by white actors and actresses.

- Government has unfairly given the advantage in all its entitlement programs to minorities and illegal aliens who were being supported by taxes paid by the white majority. Correctly or not, whites feel they have been shunned by their government (though actual numbers of recipients of all forms of government aid are white), however, in percentage numbers, minorities far surpass whites as low income recipients due to the fact more whites are not impoverished by percentage rates.
- As the white middle class diminishes due to the forces of international trade treaties, outsourcing and rapid globalization that has stripped Americans of their job security, government has done little to restore their faith in their financial stability.
- Religious conservatives who are typically Republicans want to repeal "Rowe vs. Wade" that gave women the right to have abortions. The killing of viable fetuses is considered murder if due to homicide, except in the case of women who the Supreme Court had ruled have the right to regulate the procreative process in their own bodies, and it's not the right of the state to intervene in her personal anatomical decisions.
- White men who have suffered job losses that were once proudly worked from generation to generation have good reason to feel angry at their government for selling out to foreign interests.

Chapter 5
The Art of the Meal

Trump promises better days ahead, and already Wall Street investors have been optimistic a Trump presidency will translate into great stock market profits. Already, the DOW has had more than increased the value of 401k's more than 10% as it broke the 20,000 milestone for the first time in history after reaching an all time high on 12/20/16 or 19,974. This optimism smells like and spells future job security for Americans. Even those who supported Clinton are mustering hope and faith in Trump to restore American jobs and to regain the respect of the world in products made in the U.S.A. again.

The strengthening to America's manufacturing sector to augment its vibrant technology sector would restore needed jobs to underemployed regions in the U.S. This success will galvanize the loyalty of economic beneficiaries to further trust, believe, and love President Donald J. Trump more and more with each paycheck. Average Americans who gain well paying will feel gratitude in Trump's economic plans and will not likely abandon him for uncertainties that could lead to job losses.

The DOW has surpassed all expectations, and within the first year of Donald Trump's presidency, it had soared above 26,000 for an all-time record. How long can investor optimism continue considering the North Korea crisis?

Chapter 6
The Art of the Zeal

President Trump's constituents are passionate about their values, whether that is religious morals, family life, or traditional white culture. They have political zeal, political clout and have been responsible for maintaining a Republican majority in Congress. If President Trump is successful at maintaining the loyalty of his electorate as he has already shown during the election, he has formidable and passionate political capital that he will be able to spend to support his agenda. If President Trump doubles down on his bet, he will be able to parlay his staunch support to make the Republican Congress give in to his agenda.

The maintenance of a zealous political base is essential to insure unobstructed implementation of President Trump's policies that include building the U.S./Mexico border wall and the mass deportation of undocumented residents, beginning with criminals. Conservative white Republicans are by far more patriotic and jingoistic than multiracial Democrats, and they provide the necessary ammunition to support any future war mongering decisions that Trump might implement to build up the U.S. military to protect U.S. global economic interests (including those of over 500 companies where Trump is a stakeholder).

A brief scan of human civilizations shows the routine rise of authoritarian kings, emperors, czars, sultans, caliphs, and pharoses. The U.S. Constitution permits Congress and the states to approve changes through the amendment process. Is it totally impossible for Trump's electoral troops to blindly support his domestic and foreign policies, even though the government intelligence, military and economic experts may otherwise advise him? President Trump appears to be his own man, beholden to none except his loyal electorate. He was elected with little formal assistance from his own party.

President Trump is legally exempt from many laws that govern commoners and other public officials. He need not make his private business dealings transparent to the public. He is exempt from conflict of interest laws, unless it can be proven he peddles influence for monetary gain, which he is not going to do because he has more money than anyone who might gain from his future policies. Donald Trump made his fortune from legitimate business practices, and even though people routinely sue his companies, that's just part and parcel to doing business in a competitive market climate. He is not required by law to divest his business interests, and it would be a monumental legal task to even attempt to do so for more than 500 corporations where he has financially invested. President Trump's fortunes are likely to grow, and a decade after completing his two terms, he could become the first living trillionaire the world has ever seen.

Chapter 7
The Art of War

A classical Chinese war strategy manual that is still required reading in all U.S. military colleges is *The Art of War*. President Trumps best seller, *The Art of the Deal* borrows several principles from this book of strategic thinking and positioning that Trump has used to build his financial empire. During the sometimes vicious Presidential campaign where mudslinging, accusations, and misinformation typically trumped discussion of issues that concerned voters, Trump often took to early morning "tweets" to counter attack those who criticized him on national media. Trump admitted that he attacked those who attacked him first, and it is likely his foreign policy will reflect this basic war tactic. What is unclear is how much emphasis President Trump will place on pre-emptive strikes to fulfill his vision of winning at all costs.

Following are several classic war strategy quotes from *The Art of War* by Sun Tzu. Is there any evidence that President Trump's playbook may reflect the strategic thinking both in his bestseller, The Art of the Deal, and in the battle strategies contained in The Art of War? In many ways, aren't competitive business strategies like going to war against the competition, with the goal of emerging as the clear winner?

- Appear weak when you are strong, and strong when you are weak." *The candidate Trump appeared strong when most political pundits had already counted him out.*

- "The supreme art of war is to subdue the enemy without fighting." *In the televised debates, Trump never threw a punch.*

- "If you know the enemy and know yourself, you need not fear the result of a hundred battles. If you know yourself but not the enemy, for every victory gained you will also suffer a defeat. If you know neither the enemy nor yourself, you will succumb in every battle." *We now know in retrospect that candidate Trump knew his own strengths and the weaknesses of his competitors.*

- "Let your plans be dark and impenetrable as night, and when you move, fall like a thunderbolt." *Trump's answer to media questions about how he would defeat ISIS was to say he would not announce it because that would give the enemy advanced warnings of his tactics and be able to prepare against them.*

- "Supreme excellence consists of breaking the enemy's resistance without fighting." *Trump never surrendered even when the betting odds seemed against him. He was steadfast and wore down his opponent who had to make that dreaded call of surrender.*

- "Victorious warriors win first and then go to war, while defeated warriors go to war first and then seek to win" *Yes, Trump is all about winning, but primarily through negotiation. He need not go to war to win.*

- "All warfare is based on deception. Hence, when we can attack, we must seem unable; when using our forces, we must appear inactive; when we are near, we must make the enemy believe we are far away; when far away, we must make him believe we are near." *Trump is not a simple mind, but rather clever in his business dealings that have translated to political acumen that caught his opponents with their hands down.*

- "If your enemy is secure at all points, be prepared for him. If he is in superior strength, evade him. If your opponent is temperamental, seek to irritate him. Pretend to be weak, that he may grow arrogant. If he is taking his ease, give him no rest. If his forces are united, separate them. If sovereign and subject are in accord, put division between them. Attack him where he is unprepared, appear where you are not expected." *Trump's debate performances showed his varied temperaments that seemed to irk his opponents, and he made forceful attacks and counter attacks whenever his opponents attempted to project strength.*

- "In the midst of chaos, there is also opportunity" *President Trump knows this well, and has made several friendly "tweets" to Russian President Putin.*
- "The greatest victory is that which requires no battle." *Candidate Trump on the stump was popular and victorious in garnering the support of his constituents.*
- "Engage people with what they expect; it is what they are able to discern and confirms their projections. It settles them into predictable patterns of response, occupying their minds while you wait for the extraordinary moment — that which they cannot anticipate." *It has been stated many times by political pundits that candidate Trump was a "loose cannon" and it was impossible to predict what might come out of his mouth in expressing his beliefs and those who voted to support him.*
- "Thus, we may know that there are five essentials for victory: *The following points sound much akin to business acumen in the routinely competitive global marketplace.*

  1 He will win who knows when to fight and when not to fight.

  2 He will win who knows how to handle both superior and inferior forces.

  3 He will win whose army is animated by the same spirit throughout all its ranks.

4 He will win who, prepared himself, waits to take the enemy unprepared.

5 He will win who has military capacity and is not interfered with by the sovereign."

- "There is no instance of a nation benefitting from prolonged warfare." *How could Trump not be aware of the lessons of the more than decade long Iraq War?*

- "The art of war is of vital importance to the State. It is a matter of life and death, a road either to safety or to ruin. Hence it is a subject of inquiry which can on no account be neglected." *All Presidents are keenly aware of America's national interests and the ultimate need to insure the safety and survival of America.*

Following are additional quotes from the Art of War that may shed some light on President Trump's mindset.

- "Move swift as the Wind and closely-formed as the Wood. Attack like the Fire and be still as the Mountain."
- "Treat your men as you would your own beloved sons. And they will follow you into the deepest valley."
- "When the enemy is relaxed, make them toil. When full, starve them. When settled, make them move."
- "When you surround an army, leave an outlet free. Do not press a desperate foe too hard."

Chapter 8
The Trumpets Sound

The religious Christian conservatives and evangelists are familiar with the Book of Revelations, the last book in the New Testament in the Bible. Our world continues to sit on the precipice of nuclear annihilation that could be spawned by future conflict between nuclear powers, perhaps starting as a small conflict then escalating and spreading like a wild fire until much is consumed in the conflagration. The Bulletin of the Atomic Scientist have set the "Doomsday Clock" at 3 minutes to midnight, translating to the risk of an imminent nuclear war that could be sparked by regional and international conflicts that could easily spin out of control. If fact, there have been literally hundreds of "false alarms" since the Cuban Missile Crisis when John F. Kennedy was President of the U.S.A.

President Trump is a winner, and he is not weak but is strong and appears to be willing for America to "go it alone" as in the past before withdrawal from Vietnam under President Nixon who was deposed after a scandal that would not likely take a man like Donald Trump down. However, let's for a moment look at a possible, but hopefully improbable Biblical account of what might occur should the *trumpets sound*.

Book of Revelations, Chapter 8 {excerpted with interpretation}

[2] And I saw the seven angels which stood before God; and to them were given seven trumpets.

[6] And the seven angels which had the **seven trumpets** prepared themselves to sound.

[7] The **first** angel sounded, and there followed hail and fire mingled with blood, and they were cast upon the earth: and the third part of trees was burnt up, and all green grass was burnt up. *{a nuclear explosion in a large city?}*

[8] And the **second** angel sounded, and as it were a great mountain burning with fire was cast into the sea: and the third part of the sea became blood; *{a large nuclear warhead flaming as it re-enters Earth's atmosphere, exploding over a sea in the Middle-East, likely the Red Sea?}* [9] And the third part of the creatures which were in the sea, and had life, died; and the third part of the ships were destroyed.

[10] And the **third** angel sounded, and there fell a great star from heaven, burning as it were a lamp, and it fell upon the third part of the rivers, and upon the fountains of waters; [11] And the name of the star is called Wormwood: and the third part of the waters became wormwood; and many men died of the waters, because they were made bitter. *{the fiery re-entry of a multiple nuclear warhead falling from space, exploding over rivers, possible the Tigris-Euphrates rivers in Iraq/Syria}*

[12] And the **fourth** angel sounded, and the third part of the sun was smitten, and the third part of the moon, and the third part of the stars; so as the third part of them was darkened, and the day shone not for a third part of it, and the night likewise. *{a solar and lunar eclipse, followed by smoke from the previous nuclear explosions darkening one-third of the night sky}*

Book of Revelations, Chapter 9

[1] And the **fifth** angel sounded, and I saw a star fall from heaven unto the earth: and to him was given the key of the bottomless pit. [2] And he opened the bottomless pit; and there arose a smoke out of the pit, as the smoke of a great furnace; and the sun and the air were darkened because of the smoke of the pit. *{a huge payload nuke strikes land and punctures the Earth's crust, causing the release of molten magma from the Earth's mantle, resulting in darkening the sky* [3] And there came out of the smoke locusts upon the earth: and unto them was given power, as the scorpions of the earth have power. *{the hot ash spewing from the open pit to the mantle}* [13] And the **sixth** angel sounded, and I heard a voice… Saying to the sixth angel which had the trumpet, Loose the four angels which are bound in the great river Euphrates. *{this is in Iraq/Syria}*

[15] And the four angels were loosed, which were prepared for an hour, and a day, and a month, and a year, for to slay the third part of men. [16] And the number of the army of the

horsemen were two hundred thousand thousand: and I heard the number of them. [18] By these three was the third part of men killed, by the fire, and by the smoke, and by the brimstone, which issued out of their mouths. *{one third of the 200,000,000 soldiers will be killed by battlefield explosions}*

Book of Revelations, Chapter 11

[15] And the **seventh** angel sounded; and…

[16] And he causeth all, both small and great, rich and poor, free and bond, to receive a mark in their right hand, or in their foreheads: [17] And that no man might buy or sell, save he that had the mark, or the name of the beast, or the number of his name. [18] Here is wisdom. Let him that hath understanding count the number of the beast: for it is the number of a man; and his number is Six hundred threescore and six. *{the Mark of the Beast in computer code through a bar code or chip implant with everyone's financial information encoded to permit cashless retail transactions?}*

The Bible clearly predicts many dire catastrophes during the "End Times" that may or may not happen during our lifetimes, during this generation, or never at all. Was Donald Trump fated to become President of the United States of America to play his important role in fulfilling the Biblical prophecy in the Bible's Book of Revelation? Only time will tell if this happens by 2024, presuming Trump runs and wins a second term.

I truly hope, and I'd go out on a limb to state that I have confidence President Trump will become one of the best and progressive U.S. Presidents of all time. I believe President Trump will be concerned about his legacy, because HIS FAMOUSLY BRANDED NAME is the PRODUCT most investors invest in, and probably not in his tweets, diatribes, or rants. However, his unpredictability makes for gamesmanship.

I truly hope President Trump will demonstrate that wealthy people, particularly billionaires, have within their power and resources to better the world, their nations, and their people. Perhaps the eventual growth of wealth into political power that serves the people would become the new political paradigm of benevolent leadership? The opposite result could be the growth of oligarchies and authoritarianism, which Americans of all persuasions, classes, race, religion, and ethnic groups would not likely support. Perhaps the rich could do well to adopt impoverished nations and reshape them into economic successes. Wouldn't that be great?

What if President Trump can negotiate friendly relations with our major competitors, Russia on the military front, and China on the economic front? What if having both Russia and China as American allies, President Trump will be able to build a coalition to bring lasting peace and prosperity to America and the rest of the world? This is not an impossible task, and President Trump has shown he clearly has muster to tackle what appears to be improbable tasks. God bless President Trump and America, and the rest of the world with peace.

President Trump's ultimate test is not found in domestic policies, but in dealing with the North Korean tyrannical despot Kim Jong-Un. It's amazing that all of humanity's survival hangs in the balance on Trump's decisions regarding waging a defensive, reactive, or pre-emptive war against the North Korean regime. The entire world's future hangs in the balance.

While the U.S. administrations have supported efforts to restrain nuclear proliferation, there are now many nations capable of engaging in tactical nuclear warfare that could drag America, NATO, Russia and China into the madness of nuclear conflagration that will surely kill over a billion people, and result in the collapse of the global economic system. The fortunes of the elites will be decimated, except for the military-industrial complex.

Rebuilding what radioactive world is left is uncertain as the EMP's from massive atmospheric nuclear detonations will wipe out modern day technologies. Those of the privileged classes who have advanced warning to hide in underground cities will eventually have to return to the radioactive surface world with long-term negative health consequences.

The problem with hostile rhetoric between the U.S. and North Korea sets the stage for "accidents" that could trigger a full on nuclear engagement. Perhaps it's time to recognize the North Korean regime is now a nuclear power and negotiate to remove economic sanctions for a long-term peace where it permits international inspectors to verify its limitation on developing more nukes and ICBM's. Otherwise it's GAME ON.

The fate of humanity now rests with one man... Donald Trump